The Poetry Deal

The Poetry Deal

Diane di Prima

Poet Laureate Series Number 5

City Lights Foundation
San Francisco

Library of Congress Cataloging-in-Publication Data
Di Prima, Diane.
 [Poems. Selections]
The poetry deal / Diane Di Prima.
    pages cm. — (San francisco poet laureate series ; 5)
 ISBN 978-1-931404-15-0 (paperback)
 I. Title.

PS3507.I68A6 2014
811'.54—dc23

2014023852

City Lights Books are published at the City Lights Bookstore
261 Columbus Avenue, San Francisco, CA 94133
www.citylights.com

For all my Teachers

CONTENTS

INAUGURAL ADDRESS

I want to say thanks to all the folks who nominated me
and made me Poet Laureate but I decided that to name
all those folks gets to be a litany, and really finally I would
have to say thank you to all sentient beings.

(Laughter/applause)

There isn't a thing that's happened that hasn't
helped put each of us where we are, so thanks
everybody!

This is what I've written for us:

When I came to San Francisco in 1961, I came
to a magical place—a city of bright air and beveled
glass, of jazz and poets—stained glass windows tucked
above the front door in even the poorest neighbor-
hoods, and vistas of bay and hills and sailboats that
took my breath away while I waited for a bus.

I moved here in 1968. I brought with me fourteen
grown-ups (so-called) and all their accompanying kids
& pets, horns & typewriters, and at least one rifle. We
moved from the Hotel Albert on University Place and
10th Street in Manhattan to a fourteen-room house
on the Panhandle of Golden Gate Park—a house with
an in-law apartment, a two-car garage and a garden,
that I'd rented for $300 a month.

I came away from a city where I'd run the New York
Poets Theatre and Poets Press, and produced the mim-
eographed newsletter *The Floating Bear,* first with my

lover, LeRoi Jones, and later when I left him and married someone else, alone. Roi resigned. He said it was for "personal reasons".

But New York was a city that had by that time grown too harsh, too hard to live in. A city in which I'd seen too many deaths. I came to new dreams: to a choice to be active, to *actualize* what in New York I'd only been able to write about. I came here to work in new ways for change: the grace of possibility that had opened on this coast.

Because in the New York of the 1950s, where I came of age as a poet, one wrote one's dreams, but didn't try to make them happen. To bring about what *could be*.

I'd like to read a poem I wrote back then when I decided to go ahead and have a baby, to be a single mom. "Song for Baby-o, Unborn", written for Jeanne, my first child, in early 1957. I was 22.

Sweetheart
when you break thru
you'll find
a poet here
not quite what one would choose.

I won't promise
you'll never go hungry
or that you won't be sad
on this gutted
breaking

globe
but I can show you
baby
enough to love
to break your heart
forever

I can't tell you how many young mothers have written to me, emailed me, about this poem in the years since.

I grew up in the world of McCarthy, of the death of the Rosenbergs and of Wilhelm Reich, of endless witch-hunts. I remember to this day where I was sitting—it was on the steps of the New School for Social Research—when I got the news that the Rosenbergs had been executed. I was 18. I had dropped out of college that year, and was living on the Lower East Side.

You trusted very few, and you trusted them with your life. You never talked politics or sex in public, or talked about a lot of the literature you were actually reading. I worked for years in a bookstore where you'd better know the customer well if you were going to pull out a copy of Jean Genet or even Henry Miller, when he or she asked—they were illegal.

I'm going to read a poem from the early 1960s, when I had a theater which was busted for showing the Jean Genet film *Le Chant d'Amour*. It's one of five silly theatre poems I wrote that season.

THEATRE POEM #1

How can I be serious when there are so many cops at the
                                                    door
threatening me with papers or asking to see my papers
like in a Merle Oberon movie, but I don't feel glamorous
would you, if you hadn't washed your hair in a month
or combed it in a week for that matter?

Logan Smiley says Alan's a genius, Jimmy Waring
hates everything we do, but continues to do it with us
They keep stealing Ray Johnson's pictures out of the lobby
and changing the front door lock

Well, we've been here thru a blizzard, a raid & a rainstorm
so I guess we're here to stay, the same old people
keep coming back every weekend to see the same plays
                                                    [1963]

I had begun writing poetry when I was seven. I
never stopped, but I was twice that age—fourteen—
when I gave myself wholeheartedly to the poem. I
had been reading Keats' letters, reading Shelley and
Thomas Wolfe with my friends, while going to a high
school that frowned on all things Romantic, when
I had a kind of epiphany. My mind moved in an in-
stant from hero-worship, gazing upward, to peership,
looking straight on. I realized there was no reason I
couldn't do what these folks had done. No reason I
couldn't at least try. At that moment I made what I
knew would be a life-long commitment.

From then onward for many years I didn't let a
day go by without writing.

Poetry became the guiding force in my life. It led me a few years later to drop out of college and find an apartment on what was then the Lower East Side.

Poetry led me to study ancient Greek, to visit Ezra Pound in St. Elizabeth's Hospital, to found the New York Poets Theatre with my friends, to learn offset printing and raise the money to buy my Fairchild-Davidson press. (I was very proud of it. It came second-hand with a week of printing classes.)

Poetry gave me a good, rich life on the East Coast—New York City was my school, my university for many years. It was where I learned the discipline of daily work at one's craft. I learned how to look at painting, listen to music, really *see* dance.

And one day Poetry let me know for sure that it was time to move West, to my real home, San Francisco.

Let me read a poem from 1993. About forty years after I'd committed myself to poetry, it occurred to me that—although I had always imagined the artist's life to be completely pure and selfless, there actually was—and *is*—an unspoken contract between me and the Muse. So the "you" in this poem is Poetry itself.

THE POETRY DEAL *(See p 19.)*

The San Francisco I came to in 1968 was welcoming and sweet, as it was tough and scary.

"Your writing helped bring all this about," Peter Berg had said to me two months before. (I was then in San Francisco on a reading trip, staying with Lenore Kandel.) Now he said, "Come and enjoy the fruits."

It was hardly that simple and I knew it. But the possibility of actualizing some of the dreams I'd absorbed from my anarchist grandfather and hung onto ever since—the chance to actually *act* on what I believed in, to take a shot at creating the world as we dreamed it—made me eager to join these amazing folks: poets, Diggers, Panthers, Zennies, out-riders and rebels of all sorts, in the hope-filled and wild experiment that was bubbling away in this City 1968.

My way was made easier by many: Lawrence Ferlinghetti and Nancy Peters at City Lights advanced money on the *Revolutionary Letters* I had yet to finish; Michael and Joanna McClure, Lenore Kandel, Peter Coyote, Kirby Doyle and Dee-Dee Morrill, Lew Welch, Marilyn Rose, the folks at the *Oracle* and many, many others, made it clear that I and my sprawling and non-descript tribe were welcome here. That there was plenty of work to do and plenty of room for us all.

Back in New York, my friends and I indulged in some creative financing spurred on by the many assassinations in the news—remember? Remember 1968?—and a general sense of urgency in the air. I returned from a reading trip, from San Francisco, in April. By summer solstice we were all back in San Francisco, ensconced in our newly rented house on Oak Street.

REVOLUTIONARY LETTER #4

Left to themselves people
grow their hair.

Left to themselves they
take off their shoes.
Left to themselves they make love
sleep easily
share blankets, dope & children
they are not lazy or afraid
they plant seeds, they smile, they
speak to one another. The word
coming into its own : touch of love
on the brain, the ear.

We return with the sea, the tides
we return as often as leaves, as numerous
as grass, gentle, insistent, we remember
the way,
our babes toddle barefoot thru the cities of the
universe.
[1968]

The Diggers immediately put us to work. My
household was responsible for delivering free food to
25 urban communes twice a week and free fish which
was available on Saturday mornings. (Friday was fish
day in this still-Catholic city.)

Meanwhile I was writing *Revolutionary Letters* at a
fast clip and mailing them to Liberation News Service
on a regular basis; from there they went to over 200
free newspapers all over the US and Canada. I also per-
formed them, sometimes with guitar accompaniment
by Peter Coyote, on the steps of City Hall, while my
comrades handed out the *Digger Papers*, and tried to

persuade startled office workers on their way to lunch that they should drop out and join the revolution.

I had a good friend—an old buddy of Will Geer, Woody Guthrie and Pete Seeger—named Bob DeWitt. Bob was a barefoot potter. A communist millionaire who had a ranch near Mariposa. He joyfully supplied us with sides of beef and whole sheep for our larger be-ins and other shindigs. I made a few overnight trips in a pick-up truck to bring home the goodies for these occasions.

REVOLUTIONARY LETTER #11

drove across
San Joaquin Valley
with Kirby Doyle
grooving
getting free Digger meat
for Free City Convention
grooving
behind talk of Kirby's family
been here a long time
grooving
friendship renewed, neat pickup truck, we stopped
at a gas station
man uptight at the
sight of us, sight of Kirby's hair, his friendly
loose face, my hair, our dress
man surly, uptight, we drove
away brought down
(across fields of insecticide and migrant workers)
and
"Man" I said "that cat

so uptight, what's he
so uptight about, it's not
your hair, not really, it's just
what the TV tells him about hippies
got him scared, what he reads in
his magazines
got him scared, we got to
come out from behind the image
sit down with him, if he
sat down to a beer with you he'd find
a helluva lot more to say than he'll find
with the man who makes your image
he's got nothing in common
with the men who run his mind, who tell him
what to think of us"

SMASH THE MEDIA, I said,
AND BURN THE SCHOOLS
so people can meet, can sit
and talk to each other, warm and close
no TV image flickering
between them.

[1968]

It was good times. For a while the Free Bank lived
on top of my refrigerator: it was a shoebox full of
money. I never knew how much was in there. I didn't
really care. Anyone who needed cash could come
by the house and take some. Anyone who had ex-
tra that they didn't need (and there were many—rock
musicians and dealers, among others) would drop
some off. The whereabouts of the Free Bank rotated

from one Digger house to another, but the Bank itself was solvent, the shoebox was full for at least six months that I know of, which is proof enough for me that such institutions are possible. San Francisco was . . . yeah. . . [*laughter*]. Also that we might as well print our own money and forget about them, about banks. . . [*laughter*]

San Francisco was then and still is for me the place where you can take your dreams into the streets and make them happen. Make change.

I wrote this next "Letter" in a truck as I was going, was being driven, from Tassajara to a demonstration where I'd been asked to read, at UC Santa Cruz. We had just started bombing Cambodia. Yeah, Cambodia. If some of you young ones don't know what I'm talking about, that's okay. Get someone to explain later.

SAN FRANCISCO NOTE

I think I'll stay on this
earthquake fault near this
still-active volcano in this
armed fortress facing a
dying ocean &
covered w/ dirt

     while the
streets burn up & the
rocks fly & pepper gas
lays us out

    cause
that's where my friends are,

10

you bastards,   not that
you know what that means

Ain't gonna cop to it, ain't gonna
be scared no more, we all
know the same songs, mushrooms, butterflies
                                        we all
have the same babies, dig it
the woods are big.

                                        [1970]

(applause) They're still pretty big, guys.

I know because I'm told—it's been repeated to
me by all kinds of folks: on NPR by Michael Kras-
ny; it's in the paper; it's a fact of life from my poetry
students that San Francisco, even the Mission or the
Western Addition, is getting too expensive for artists.
That dancers, poets, musicians are moving somewhere
else. And every once in a while I read the paper and
realize how much of my city is now run by the UN-
PHUN Party. *(laughter)* That's spelled U-N P-H-U-
N. I call them the UnPhun Party, the Surrealists call
them Miserabilists. *(laughter)*

   They can be Democrats, Republicans, radicals—
it doesn't matter. One way you can identify them is
they don't even know how to distinguish between
noise and music, or between vandalism and art. They
just want it *out* of their neighborhood. They are afraid
people might be having a good time.

That UnPhun Party has unfortunately gotten very big in San Francisco. It can now be found on many boards and planning commissions. *(laughter)* Selling fear, selling puritanical morals, making rules about *eros*, lumping all drugs together, so that one high school kid I met while teaching told me, "I might as well shoot heroin. I'm already evil. I smoke pot."

But I'm old enough so that most of the time I suffer from the senility of star-dust in my eyes. I think they call it the beginning of cataracts. *(laughter)* I'll read you a poem from this past spring. You'll see about the stardust. It's called "Reality Is No Obstacle". *(laughter)*

REALITY IS NO OBSTACLE
for the Chicago Surrealist Group

refuse to obey
refuse to die
refuse to sleep
refuse to turn away
refuse to close your eyes
refuse to shut your ears
refuse silence while you can still sing
refuse discourse in lieu of embracement
come to no end that is not
a Beginning

And I let this stardust, these cataracts, the dust or bus-exhaust or whatever it is—I let it convince me that I live in the place I dreamed of when I came here. The place I knew San Francisco was going to grow into when I moved here over forty years ago.

I am certain of nothing but of the holiness of the Heart's affections, and the truth of Imagination, said John Keats. Remember? *What the Imagination seizes as Beauty must be truth—whether it existed before or not.*

So, a San Francisco where all sexual preferences are good, all pleasure and delight is wonder-full as long as there is joy and communication and no one cares about marriage and no one by the way wants to join the Army, any Army! W*hy would you do that?* Where no drug is criminalized, though some are more useful than others, and addictions are treated benignly and without judgment. Where everyone is taught how to use psychedelics. Even how to use pot. Just as one is taught both safety and *pleasure* in sex education and *The Mass Psychology of Fascism* by Wilhelm Reich is required reading in high school. *(laughter)* In the fifth grade kids memorize the *Universal Declaration of Human Rights.*

A San Francisco where no one is hungry and free meals are festive communal banquets, or delivered and elegantly served to those who can't or don't want to go out or eat in a crowd. Where folks are housed where and with whom they choose, because *housing is a basic human right.* Where health care is free and available in all its forms: acupuncture, western medicine, chiropractic, orgone box, hypnosis, ayurveda, magickal ritual, laying on of hands—modes I haven't even dreamed of, performed by shamans of every sex. And the healers have offices if they wish on campuses where folks are paid to play flutes or bongos under the trees and make all patients feel welcome.

The schools are full of poetry, music, painting, boat-building, farming, astronomy, jazz, sculpture, studio recording—whatever the kids deem useful and want to learn. The colleges are free and full of excitement, because the people who are there really *want* to be there and are studying only what they want to know.

A San Francisco where all empty buildings have been turned into theatres, meeting halls, performance spaces, living quarters—whatever their respective neighborhoods decide.

Where even the words "surveillance", "immigrant", "deportation" have never been spoken and everyone is welcome. Everyone shares their music, their food, their vision with everyone else. Where the words "juvenile criminal" are seen as the oxymoron they are and prisons have been abolished. Where war is a fading memory—a story told by our elders and those invasive Blue Angels have long since gone elsewhere—anywhere they're welcome, if they're still welcome anywhere at all.

Oh, did I mention that there is plenty of work? Everyone who needs or wants one has a job: people are busy fixing streets, restoring, & replanting Golden Gate Park—that jewel of our city!—and all the smaller neighborhood parks are rejuvenated, their rec centers open late into the night. Every neighborhood park has after-school fun stuff to do. Free daycare of all kinds is available. Parents and kids get to choose what works for them. Young people are busy tutoring kids, caring for, visiting, amusing, learning from the old. The disabled are using their many skills. They have friends, they feel valued, a part of our social fabric.

People are painting murals, playing music, making art everywhere and being paid for it. Muni & BART are free as are the ferry boats. Cinemas, theatres, museums *[applause]* opera and jazz concerts—all free.

Of course there are jobs on the welcoming committees. Young musicians and artists and crafts-people when they arrive are welcomed and given housing and supplies and a stipend for food and clothing. They are given a map of the places where they can perform, or show their work, print their books. Communal graphics studios and art studios are in every neighborhood.

[Pause]

What happened folks?

This is where we were heading. How did we allow ourselves to be derailed? So badly derailed that I read in the *Chronicle* last week that if you can't pay your rent in this town and you have school-age kids, you won't be evicted until the school year ends—how stupid is that?

"School's out! Yayy! Goody! . . . . uh, uh! All our stuff's in the street, there's a lock on our door. . . . now mom is crying. . . ." What kind of human passes a rule like that?

They're even waffling on, or have completely dropped by now, our long-held policy of *sanctuary*—used to be a sacred word—remember? Sanctuary. Asylum. For so-called "illegal immigrants".

My peeps—I am ashamed to be one of you.

(silence)

And it's not just our town, it's the country as a whole. Now we've suspended medical evacuations from Port-au-Prince till it's clear who's going to pay. Even the Borg behaved better. At least to their own species. My friends—I am ashamed of who we are. What we've become.

(tears)

Well, that ain't my San Francisco. Not the San Francisco I am Poet Laureate of. I owe my allegiance to poetry and to the people of this city. I owe my allegiance to the City I came to—*that* San Francisco. City of sunlight bounced off ocean and bay, city of kindness: of people who have time—time to look each other in the eye. Time to listen, to bear witness to each others' lives.

I'd like to read one more poem. When I wrote it, I was already Poet Laureate, but nobody had announced anything. We were waiting on Mayor Newsom. Then Jack Hirschman asked me to read at the International Poetry Festival he curates here every other year.

FIRST DRAFT: POET LAUREATE
OATH OF OFFICE
for all poets everywhere

It is the poem I serve
luminous, through time
that celebration
of human breath,   of *melos*

it is and always has been
the muse   androgynous and ruthless
as any angel   scattering words   that need no
radio frequency   no broadband

it is the light on the ocean here and
the sky   in all its moods
luminous fog that wakes me up
to write,   and something I call the
"Imp of the Short Poem"

it is the people of San Francisco
in their beauty
Bright luminous eyes   looking out
from homeless faces

looking up
from gardening   skateboarding   singing
playing cards   playing ball
barbecuing in their backyards

the folks in the Mission
the Excelsior   in Bayview
Hunters Point

Japantown
North Beach
folks in the Sunset
working & idle
passionate   angry   silent
powerful in their silence

my friends and neighbors
parked at Ocean Beach, at Twin Peaks
in their cars
watching the sun go
                        down

my vow is:

to remind us all
to celebrate
there is no time
too desperate
no season
that is not
a Season of Song

[2009]

THE POETRY DEAL

I want to say that I don't want anything
but the whisper of yr scarf as you do
the Dance of the Seven Veils
soft sound of yr satin slippers on the carpet
and the raw, still bloody meat you toss my way
that I chew on, all night long.

I don't want anything you don't already give me:
trips to other worlds,   dimensions of light
or sound,   rides on the back of a leopard
on those black rocks, high over
some sea or gorge.   But it isn't true

I want all that,   sheet lightning of quasars
that you dance between, those colors, yes,
but I want you as mother, sister
stone walls of the cave I lie in
in trance for seven days,   the mist around my cabin
that makes it invisible.

I want the flare & counterpoint of words
& I want the non-verbal—what never can be spoken
as a foundation.
                    I'd like my daily bread
however you arrange it, and I'd also like
to *be* bread, or sustenance, for some others
                    even after

I've left. A song they can walk a trail with.

I don't think we talked abt money or success
or fame, whatever that is—for a long time
I hoped you'd forget that part, now I'll do as you say
about all that. Whatever seems most useful.

I'd like to keep learning how to brew bitter herbs
& how to make them translucent, edible
                              almost crystalline.

What I offered *you* wasn't much: you can always wake
                                              me
Like my closest friend,   or most loved lover.

You can burn my favorite snapshot of myself
Lead me on paths or non-paths anywhere
You can not make sense for years & I'll still believe
                                              you
drop husbands, tribes & jobs as you wish

You mostly aren't jealous—have taken yr place
alongside gardens, bread-making, children, printing
                                              presses
But when yr eyes shoot sparks & you say
"Choose between me & *it*"—"it" has always gone
Except when "it" was my kids
I took that risk
& we worked it out somehow

Now I've come to a place
where there are no kids, no tribe, no bread, no
                                                garden
only you in your two faces: formed & formless.
Nothing to hold back now
& nothing to offer.

I stand before you: a piece of wind
w/a notebook & pen

which one of us is it dances?
and which is the quasar?

CITY LIGHTS 1961

Going there for the first time
it was so much smaller then
that crowded downstairs full of poetry
racks of tattered little mags against the wall
those rickety white tables where folks sat reading/
writing
Vesuvio's was like an adjunct office

Arriving again a year later, two kids in tow
Lawrence gave me a huge stack of his publications
"I've got books" he said "like other people have
mice"

And North Beach never stopped being mysterious
when I moved out here in 1968
that publishing office on Filbert & Grant was a mecca
a place to meet up with my kids if we got separated
during one of those innumerable demonstrations
(tho Lawrence worried, told me I shd keep them
out of harm's way, at home) *I* thought they shd learn
whatever it was we were learning—
Office right around the corner from the bead store
where I found myself daily, picking up supplies

How many late nights did we haunt the Store
buying scads of new poems from all corners of the
earth

then head to the all-night Tower Records full of
                                        drag–queens
& revolutionaries, to get a few new songs

And dig it, City Lights still here, like some old
                                        lighthouse
though all the rest is gone,
the poetry's moved upstairs, the publishing office
right there now too   & crowds of people
one third my age or less still haunt the stacks
seeking out voices from all quarters
of the globe

FOR PIGPEN

Velvet at the edge of the tongue,
at the edge of the brain, it was
velvet.   At the edge of history.

Sound was light.   Like tracing
ancient letters w/yr toe on the
floor of the ballroom.
They came & went, hotel guests
like the Great Gatsby.
And wondered at the music.
                    Sound was light.

jagged sweeps of discordant
Light.   Aurora borealis over
some cemetery.   A bark.   A howl.

At the edge of history & there was
                    no time.

shouts.   trace circles
of breath.   All futures.   Time
was this light & sound
spilled out of it.

Flickered
& fell under blue windows. False dawn.
And too much wind.

We come round.
Make circles.   Blank as a clock.
Spill velvet damage at the edge
of history.

MISSING THE GRATEFUL DEAD

it was not the crowd in the sunshine
that I missed
ten thousand faces lit
by the afternoon
nor the sinuous California
rock

it was not that I missed you
   (I always
   miss you)
but—

      I waited
till yr voice on the phone
released me

I waited for yr voice
            & the light
slanted
    & failed

not to be touched
or to be both touched
& released

that I might flow
toward the natural acts
of the day

as you flowed
                    will you wait
till I call?
                    & the light fades
& fog flows

back
        over these hills

                                    [May 22, 1982]

FILLMORE & HAYES

It never stopped being the Wild West
A different holster   different
gunfighters' stance   but that same
                    desperate taste:
blood in the mouth,   corral or
                    liquor store

It never
stopped being the Lincoln
County Wars

[Winter Solstice, 2008]

350

impenetrable as the air we will be
left with   soon the air will be
impenetrable as the ground. The basis or
foundation call it. we think what's under
our feet dependable. we are too eager

to try it, stand on it,   "stand
up, stand up for your rights"   we
sang not long ago. now the ground
melts and shifts it won't support us,
support our weight. watch earth become mud

spherical mudslide slithering over magma core, see
the green ice flicker,   shrink and disappear.
Wish you were here. I do so
wish dodo bird was here,   wish orangutan
red man of alchemy was here to

stay, like our love, wish the taiga,
the Siberian tiger, Great Barrier reef and
all the rest of it would hang
around, like those brave desperate warriors of
New Zealand. *What is to be done?*

as Lenin asked. Image and body can
wake us up—as no number will.

Pitch in. Read poems at rallies. Stand
guard over plover eggs at Daytona Beach.
I keep thinking of sunrise over Greenland

from a plane. I keep thinking of
the aurora borealis, how it fits the
palm of my hand like the spotted
owl. Blue butterflies on San Bruno Mountain.
Anything at all is reason enough to

act: Eyes of your grandchild or some
ten-year-old you never met in the ghetto.
No difference. No way to know either
of them. No way to turn away.
AND DO WHAT? YOU GOT AN IDEA?

Three hundred and fifty parts per million
of *what*? We can't see them, can't
touch them, don't have any idea of
what to do with them. They don't
bare their teeth in my ancient limbic

brain. Or what you call the world's
information bloodstream. I do know no *number*
will bring us together, get us moving.
Take home a baby rhino. Undam the
Yellow River. Stop burning rainforests for food.

Dream. Pray to the elements the Five
Great Mothers, our universe. Ask more questions.

Build an ice floe for a family
of polar bears. Unplug one day a
week: stay home tell stories make love

Note: I wrote "350" soon after the launch of the 350.org web-
site, at the request of Rebecca Solnit. It is hard to write a poem
to order. Also, there was the added problem that scientific facts
make for lousy poems. I knew I would have to to trick myself.
I opened my notebook and made a scaffold, a grid that would
hold 350 words: ten stanzas, each five lines long, with seven
words in each line. Okay. My poem-to-be had a shape. I let
my mind hover loosely above the grid, while I focused on the
"fact": 350 parts per million of carbon dioxide in the atmo-
sphere would spell the death of the planet—the tipping point
for life on earth. I wrote as fast as I could, filling in that grid. I
watched while the poem moved toward—and moved the reader
toward—Acts of the Imagination which anyone could Do /or
Image / in the course of a day.

DEATHS: PHILIP WHALEN
June 26, 2002

Large man
great   light / down
Laguna
Honda
          large fort
          below   hill

I came
riding
thru fog
riding
          at Solstice
while the great waters
of the Pacific   move

as mist across the
land

Large man
great   light
mind
            as a beacon
across the city
across

the nation

he lay
breathing harsh
              deep
breathing   even
              no struggle
the men
gathered around a table in an
Ante-Chamber
              poets & monks
they spoke
in soft voices

the women
gathered around the bed

in the small
death chamber

              They
breathed.   He breathed
skin   dry
              hot
                   one woman
poet
       moistened
his dry lips

              The great man

motionless
        His breath

like slow   even   steps

as you come to
end of a path

emerge
         from trees

look over
        the cliff's edge

A SHORT HISTORY OF BYZANTIUM
for Will Alexander

The end of the 12th century found Europe in
                                        confusion
like an ice-bound tornado.
Not that the emperor was entirely inactive
& I am not speaking of mechanics here.

Like an ice-bound tornado
he inherited a desperate situation.
I am not speaking only of mechanics.
It remained for the Saracen to mop up.

He inherited a desperate situation
as if floating thru black electrical sand.
It would remain for the Saracens to mop up
and redefine their enclosures by utterance

while floating thru black electrical sand.
The news of the fall of Jerusalem reached the West.
It redefined the enclosure.
Thus the Emperor's decomposing remains were
                                        hastily buried.

When the news of the fall of Jerusalem reached the
                                        West
floating before all eyes like bits of amber or blood,

the Emperor's decomposing remains had been hastily
buried
appearing & disappearing at a trapezoidal crossroads.

Flashing before all eyes like blood & amber
& launched simultaneously from land & sea
there appeared at once at a trapezoidal crossroads—
the long Venetian ships riding low in the water.

What was launched simultaneously from land and
sea?
Think of it all as a ruthless anti-ballet
with those Venetian ships riding low off-shore
and shifting thru different centigrades & spectrums.

Yes, think if you will of a ruthless anti-ballet
where not even the emperor could be entirely
inactive.
Then shift the tale thru various measures and *spectra*:
Twelfth Century Europe was indeed in a *lot* of
confusion.

[with lines from John Julius Norwich
and Will Alexander]

ALCHEMICAL SIGNALS

for instance, the aurora borealis
lightning,   a beached whale
the dream you didn't have   or
a slip of the tongue

these are *signs*
(everyone else is telling stories)

signs can't be told
tho you can learn
to read them—

if you're lucky enough to
catch one going by

keep it to yourself

LINGUISTICS

Everywhere I go
language has preceded me
like a lover preparing the way
like an empire I cannot escape.

The narrowest canyons have their pictographs
just above the level of the waters
& the waters are not silent either.

The act of language has left its mark on the stars.
It has filled space w/myriad tiny mirrors
reflecting some inner movement.

Wherever I set my feet I hear the rustle
of the passage of dialect & ancient form
& language like some great magnetic river
flows thru the valleys & over the peaks of the world.

NOVEMBER 2, 1972
(for Ezra Pound)

remember I visited you
              at "St. Liz"
yr civil talk; the ravings of madmen around you

you handed me stolen food as I left
saying "line those stomachs"
saying "poets have to eat"
and walked me courteously to yr door
and waited for the warden to unlock it.

OCTOBER!
for Ammiel & for Ana

Too many times   back in the day   sang   *We shall*
overcome   & of course   we shan't.   Shall
not.   That's just more Puritan BS
Not overcome.   &
Nobody needs to
But we still try—or I do. I struggle
to get it *right*.
                    Goodbye, September!   Goodbye
Back to School!   New ugly clothes, crisp socks &
notebooks, sharpened pencils.

It's October—the month the veil
grows thin   &   this entire world
becomes threshold   w/ angel (or daemon)
sitting on either side.   October when death
is a *fait accompli*.   October, you herald
November, when no one struggles

                                    anymore

in the rain—we turn ourselves over
to mist   remembrance   black & white movies
            like *Atalante*   we become
mist—look over our own shoulders   regret (again)
our cruelties,   turn to salt,   melt
in the rain   or wait
till December brings Return   *Sol Invictus*

that's NOT   Soul   you know
not   s – o – u – l

Spirit (I guess)   Tibetans
call it "mind-stream"   the breath
moves outward   *that* continues
for better or worse.   but   *Sol*
Invictus descends
at the height of Her power   returns
into Dark.   *stop thinking*

about it   my friend writes   *watch*
the ballgame.   I wake in white
morning fog,   go about my business—*lay*
down my sword & shield.
                        Can't struggle to see
what will be clear   someday   can't fight
my way thru this dark wood.   Not now.
Lay down.   Watch the ballgame.

It's October baseball   again.   It's Brooklyn
1949   &   *I'll*
be down to get you   if the body
(my higher power now)   steps on
                        that plane
        Ain't gonna study war   you know
I can't

        been too long in the wind
        too long in the rain   can't fight

my ultimate lover   empty space
    Light I came in with

                    ain't gonna
study   *war*
                        at home or
in the field   ain't gonna
overcome
          no   more

[October 3, 2010]

I DREAM OF
AMY EVANS **&** MICHAEL MCCLURE
THE NIGHT BEFORE THEIR WEDDING

I see you stand in a kitchen
on a simple morning

all ages   faces   dress

I see your eyes exchange a single light
which says & says again

> *love is the immortality*
> *we carry with us*

WISTERIA LIGHT

In the early days of eternity when none of us was naked as yet, and a good thing too, I opted to plaster the back stairs. Not that the stairs wanted to be plastered, but I was certain that was the only way the billiard table would fit. Workmen dropped hammers here & there. You were vacuuming, by god, though the plaster wasn't dry, as if you were going to get an A for neatness. There were two slots in this greeting card, a kind of microchip it was, with Franz Kline wiring, not that we thought then that black & white would be a problem even for the moon. Our returning to the same haven as uncertain as coming out each time in a different one. No one distinguished between the blessed & the unblessed, no immortals had immigrated here for some time. I wanted to order wisteria, something to mitigate the light in those canyons. When you wisely pointed out it wouldn't grow there, I thought to murder you with the pail with which you were mopping the windows. I clearly saw brick walls, the red mellowing to yellow, or brown shingle shadowed with the ancient vines. I wanted none of those we had invited, whoever they were. Or the flat light they loved. I saw that clearly. Return to the present was an unhappy business, saturated as it was with murdered swallows. *I Vesperi Siciliani* slid into one slot, and I was afraid Pagliacci would find the other. And there we would be, like the king who drives his chariot around & around in that tiny courtyard, circles of paving stones without even a pear tree. Stuck as a crow on a telephone pole, once you've seen it, the pole is never again empty, there's always a crow, black in your mind's eye in front of the white sky before sunrise.

FOG: SAN FRANCISCO

it grows dark
at lunchtime
in this land of no summer

POSTCARD FROM MARSHALL, CA

floodtides
creep right *up to*
these houses on the Bay
tide covers the road & leaves a thin layer of mud

green-slippery-molding-thick-crazy-wetness bursting
into
narcissus, ferns, pale grass like green velvet elf-cloth
this North Coast a huge compost pile, alive w/one
million mushrooms
(all one mushroom)
whales go by at the Point, leaping & spouting for our
binoculars
"Minus Tides" uncover the fat, lazy clams
who only get uncovered twice a year
Bullfrog jubilation! Slugs & snails glisten on slimy
porches
Thick moss green on stacked firewood

And all the clothes in the closet smell of mildew

LOT'S WIFE DOESN'T HAVE

a name.   Whether she turned
            or not

is not the question. It's rather
who was she—what
did she look like?   (before she
turned—if she *did* turn—into that
pillar   of salt)   how

did he greet her   when she
came in from the fields?

KIRBY DOYLE

we live in true relation to the people
we live in true relation to the earth
—American Indian prayer

now Kirby's gone
at whose house
Freddie Herko
    &
George Herms
        wd play

we live long
    enuf
we live

in true relation

[April 5, 2003]

ON THE TRAIN

1.

green shack in Richmond
"Merlin's" painted on the door

just that

2.

"Halfway to Baghdad"
says the headline.   The graffiti
reads   "Whitey Repent"

at least the Bay Bridge snapped
Maybe because the people
haven't. They just keep going:
dopey smiles,   dopey music in
their ear buds.   *Somebody*
had to say something

& the dolphins, if they tried,
wouldn't be believed

ESCAPES

I thought I was teaching
Thought I knew *some*thing
Till she came to my door, one kid
in a stroller, one toddler   held
her hand
            Where she wanted to know
shd she run? Chernobyl had just
                        happened
the wind had changed, the FALLOUT
was moving across the Pacific

& this young mother
                    her tiny
wad of cash   her broke-down
car   prepared to drive
to take her kids
                    to safety
ready to

OUTRUN THE WIND

TO A STUDENT

POEMS ARE ANGELS
come to bring you
the letter you wdn't
              sign for

earlier, when it was
           delivered
by yr life

DOMINIQUE

when she was eight
we took her to the zoo

I'm really glad she said
I saw a rhinoceros
so I can tell my children
it wasn't a myth

MAX ERNST IN SUBURBIA

screw the hammer tighter
into the eyeballs of the lemonade
of discipline

repair the front porch
with the bones   of Big Foot

his children
watch you   from the trees
you planted   on the edge

of your purple lawn

GERI'S GARDEN
Petaluma

plaster ducks in
dry fountain   windfall apples
annunciation lilies wilting in
late August sun
fuchsias & driftwood
airplane noises
women writing in broken
chairs   in the shade
geraniums saying   *wait till*
next year   silk roses
in white pot
neighbor's dog barks
at empty   wicker
birdcage
stones   sea-glass
abalone   all
tumbled together   a raven
caws.   Tin lantern in plum
tree.   The ivy is
planning to take over
the world.   Non-functional
watering can,   painted
w/ hearts.

GRACIAS

Escape from dry New College lecture
to lunch!   Mexican music
slow & romantic   & from
my window seat thousands of kids
are walking home from school.
Woman in fake leather jacket
w/ packages precarious in baby
stroller, talks animated, the kid
peers out from under.
                           Large black
mom w/ tiny boy.   High school women
flirtatious in down jackets (it's cold).
Pour juice,   think of mangos
in warm highlands, bursting ripe
Gracias! and the thick smells
of that air.   Sip
it.   *Thank*
you so much.   Even the plastic
plant in the window bows.
Mission bus packed & a storm
is coming in   over Golden Gate
Furniture Co.   The song keeps saying
corazòn   &   a beautiful woman
brings food.   *Gracias*
I stammer, she is as gracious
as if this were her dining room.
Muchas gracias.   The corn chips

maize growing tall in desert
    blue Hopi corn
Betty brought from her Berkeley
garden   corn   (they say)
the secret of torch-lit Eleusis.
Gracias.   She brings
guacamole   I see avocados
of San Joaquin Valley. *Gracias!*
Add cheese & sour cream   see slow
black & white cows on
green California hills   *Thank you.*
gracias,   and tomatoes
brought from new world to old
so my folks could add them
to Marco Polo's noodles
from China: *et voilà!* Italian
cuisine! *Thanks. Muchas*
gracias.   Grazie
assai.   kids spin by
on bikes   Chinese man
in Oakland A's cap,   gay lad in enormous
cowboy hat,   wind coming up
young women, w/ backpacks,
rough workers' hands   two zillion
shiny Buicks thunder by   low-riders
burning oil,   the rain
is starting now   *Thanks*
very much,   the lunch
was very good.

[November 15, 1983]

CLEARING THE DESK

I'm sorry I was
sick
on the road
at the gym
on retreat
meeting a deadline
buying socks
freaked out
watching baseball
painting
grieving
when you came to town

I was too
broke
tired
busy
discouraged
dirty
unhinged
ecstatic
embarrassed
sad
desperate
to answer yr letter

in which you asked me
for a blurb
a place to stay
to come to yr reading
        concert
        garden show
to fly for free to L.A. to do a memorial
for our friend who's been dead for thirty years
        or more, I can't remember

I really meant to send poems to yr new magazine
        with the nifty name
        or to yr friend's anthology abt
        fishing
        millennia
        grandmothers
        jazz
        buddhism
        whales
        bisexuality
        modern art
        hospitality
        revolution
        tribal law
        rock n roll
        education
        dope or
        indigenous plants

I really *wanted* to
write something for that festschrift
support your union
nominate you passionately for a grant
give you permission to set all my work to music
        composed by interactive computers at MIT
or to tape my Beat poems in your Australian accent
        complete with didgeridoo

I'd love to send money (if I only had some) to
        the UFW
        Nalanda Translation Committee
        Greenpeace
        Project Open Hand
        the San Francisco Jazz Festival
        the Society to Lynch Newt Gingrich
        & that new one: People Against Impermanence
        (such a sweet idea)

I didn't mean to ignore you
or hurt your feelings
but if it helps at all
feel free to ignore this note
I will understand

NOTES ON THE ART OF MEMORY
for Thelonius Monk

The stars are a memory system
for thru them

              we remember our origin

Our home is behind the sun
or a divine wind

              that fills us

makes   us   think   so

MEMORIAL DAY, 2003

> *Today is Memorial Day. Take time to remember*
> *those brave souls who gave their lives for freedom.*
> *—Dear Abby*

Remember Sacco & Vanzetti
Remember Haymarket
Remember John Brown
Remember the slave revolts
Remember Malcolm
Remember Paracelsus
Remember Huey & Little Bobby Hutton
Remember Crazy Horse & Chief Joseph
Remember the Modoc & the Algonquin Nation
Remember Patrice Lumumba
Remember the dream of Africa
Remember Tina Modotti
Remember Makhnov & Tsvetaeva & Mayakovski
yes, goddammit, even remember Trotsky

Hey, do you remember Hypatia?
        Socrates? Giordano Bruno?
Remember my buddy, Esclarmonde de Foix
Remember Seton the Cosmopolite
Remember Edward Kelly, alchemist murdered in prison

Remember to take yr life back into yr hands
It's Memorial Day, remember
        what you love
 & do it—don't wait

Remember life hangs by a thread—
          anybody's life
& then remember the poets:
Shelley & Bob Kaufman

Remember Van Gogh & Pollock
Remember Amelia Earhart
Remember it's not a safe time & all the more reason
To do whole-heartedly what you have to do
Remember the women & men of Wounded Knee,
Kent State, remember where you stand :
in the midst of empire, & the Huns
are coming

Remember Vercingetorix, Max Jacob
Apollinaire & Suhrawardi, remember

that all you need to remember is what you love
Remember to Marry the World

SUNDAY MORNING SAUNA

On the stoop you can smell the sea, it fell
                              w/the rain last night
Dudes on the corner already at work
hosing their cars, little boys w/big sponges
helping out. A lady in straw hat
                              flowers on the brim
walks slowly up the hill, bible on her arm
                              tambourine in her hand.
She smiles. A bunch of little girls
pony tails tied w/big pink bows
sit on the sidewalk, getting their starched skirts
                              filthy.
The old men watch them.   Smoke, leaning on canes
                              or fences, some of them sit
on cement stoops, watching. Watching the street.

Near the park, two Doberman pinschers
                              bark at a boy
who stands on a porch, toy pistol
in his hand. Clean air comes w/ altitude:
here by Duboce Park, bottom of the hill
it smells of dog shit, you walk carefully
                              avoiding broken glass.
On the park benches thin young men are talking.
They wear stainless steel crosses on purple ribbons
                              and black clergyman's suits.
Stringy hair. Kids play in painted plaster tunnels.
                              A frisbee comes crookedly by.

Noe Valley is clean & painted & for sale.
At the sauna a woman is sleepily folding towels.
Tall girl comes in w/a pack on her back
two kids in tow, she wants a private room.
They bargain about the kids. Old man comes down
                                    the hall
his clean wet hair plastered flat from
                    Sunday bath.

[San Francisco, 1972]

MEANWHILE THE WORLD GOES DOWN

The land is inhabited by a tribe
of screeching madmen.   Who only know
the raging terror behind their eyes
and greed and greed and greed

You step out on yr porch for a minute
& are swept up
shot down
or you turn to stone:
Those are the choices

There are always choices
That's what makes us great

WAR HAIKU: Lebanon
July 2006

even an hour of this
would be too long:
white phosphorus

great lords of the Sea!
it is *Tyre* that is burning—
that harbor

don't ask why I
have bad dreams
ask why if I don't

MAY-DANCE, 2011

May the Standing Stones once more
Guard the edge of the space-time continuum
May the Maypole-dance, the dance of Life continue
May we begin the healing of our earth

May *brightnesse* cease to *fall from the aire*
May we remember who we are / who we have
                                         always been

Before "race"
Before "class"
Before "gender"
Before the past 10,000 years'
20,000 years' Stupidity
   (means being in a Stupor)

May our only struggle once again
be the ultimate struggle
within our own mind/heart
The struggle to open further

Open to all humans
To all beings
To all that is
All that can be

MAY IT BE PEACEFUL
MAY IT BE JOYOUS

ALL POWER TO THE IMAGINATION

& ABOUT OBAMA

if you were living
in the enemy's house
wife & kids there too

& guarded—all of you—
by known assassins

how hard wd *you* fight
do you think
for what were only—
after all—dreams

knowing there's no way
you'll actually win

what wd *you* be willing
—do you think—
to pay?

to see them
(those beautiful women)
walk out of there
whole
           not widowed
or orphaned

No matter what you *believed*
how much wd you
DO?

HAITI, CHILE, TIBET

LET'S STOP FOR A MOMENT TO REMEMBER WHAT WE ARE
a handful of tribes on a rather small rock
where water streams over arable earth
into larger, living waters we call "ocean"

and all is not well with our rock, it might even
                                come apart
could be it will soon be another asteroid belt
                or meteors—
                just a bunch of meteors

While our rock is shaking, and water pours from the
                                            skies
and the winds have turned demonic
could be it's time   maybe it's really time
                        to rewrite
                        the Social Contract
or at least change the rules that apply in catastrophe

Just a few suggestions:
1. ALL HANDS ON DECK
                means just that
                it's a *really* small planet

2. ANYONE BRINGING HELP ANYWHERE IT'S NEEDED
      BRINGING FOOD   BLANKETS
                WATER   MEDICINE
IS WELCOME (obviously)
don't ask where they're "from"—
        just say Thank You
(& we'd better learn to say Thank You
in hundreds of languages)

3. ALL BORDERS DISAPPEAR IN CATASTROPHE
                they are stupid & irrelevant anyway

4. THERE IS NO SUCH THING AS LOOTING IN A DISASTER
think about it—after Katrina & Rita, look back a bit
after the quakes in Chile, Haiti, Kobe, Managua—
can you call it looting when anyone breaks plate glass
        comes out with radios   medicine
        camping supplies   whatever is needed
is that looting or just plain sanity?
        keeping a family, keeping each other, alive

5. THERE IS NO PLACE FOR POLICE OR ARMY IN TRAGEDY
        except as facilitators
        distributors
UNARMED they should walk the streets, bringing
                            food
        putting out fires, digging people out
        rescuing those stranded on rooftops or bridges
                     or fleeing a flood

they shd be digging latrines
putting up shelters,
helping people find each other

6. EVERY BUILDING STILL INTACT SHD OPEN ITS DOORS
to everyone
        what else are guest rooms for?
whoever comes to your door should be taken in
        I learned when I was four
she's your guest—should be given the best
        of what you've got
even if she had been your enemy
Not special. It's a universal law
        —why we're still around at all

7. GIVE UP CONFUSING YR PROPERTY WITH YOUR LIFE
Give up confusing your property with your life.
This will save a lot of problems.
Stuff comes & goes
        & holding onto it
is like trying to hold back a river
                with your hands

8. STOP ASKING WHAT OTHERS "BELIEVE"
        just look in their eyes
        & see we are the same, they are the same
        as your most beloved child, yr dog, yr lover

no child is hungry who is not your grandchild
HOW LONG WILL YOU LET HER STARVE?
no child is orphaned who is not your son
& WHAT WILL IT TAKE
                    before we remember our own?

[Walpurgis, 2010, San Francisco]

CARTOGRAPHY

OUTER
Bow. This part
is easy.   Keep all thoughts even slightly
questionable,   to yourself.

It is probably better to
color w/in the lines
cross at the crosswalk.   Never stare
into a stranger's eyes.

On the map
assume north is
where they say it is.

INNER
feel the dance, it
never stops.   nor do
the winds.   they blow
from inside out.

Remember, there *are* 2 norths
distinguish between them

SECRET
you take
whatever direction you take.
Not out of indifference
or nonchalance.

You love the maps.
Tho they lied
they got you here.

MOST SECRET
perhaps you dreamed
the maps.   perhaps you
burned them.   Anyway
they're not here.

And north is everywhere.

THE POETRY READING

four voices   four
eras   four poetic
line(s)

        inter weave

hang
    contrapuntal
in the room

form a web
       in the

mind

in jazz   in poetry
you have to keep
    a hair
            ahead
                    of the beat

or else
you're just marking time

[City Lights May Day Reading, 2010]

KEEP THE BEAT

keep it!
was François Villon a Beat?
the Minnesingers?
what's a troubadour?

what about them guys
we call the
"Wandering Scholars" who
left the monastery
for the road?

it's not a "Generation"
dig—
     it's a state of mind

a way of living
gone on
      for centuries
a way of writing too

"Beat" poetry's older
than the *grove of academe*
older than
        Apollo
or Pythagoras

it's one of the ways
that Dionysios plays
tongues of ecstasy

"Romantic" is another
how many more
don't know

but I know for sure
it's not a "Generation"
not once
one time / **one** country

throw in your lot
w/ the gals & guys on the streets
write like you talk
talk like you sing
sing like you dance
            or love

it's a risk
        an adventure
& it plays the edge

live close to the edge
& love it
        free to fail
nothing to lose
tongues of ecstasy
no where to go

nowhere to fall but
into the arms
of the Father/Mother
the *yabyum*
        Dionysios! *Evoe!*

       [City Lights May Day Reading, 2010]

SHIRLEY HORN AT YOSHI'S

How long can music
override the pain?

She reaches for the playlist.

tender   not fragile
this tissue of connection

artists

      all ages

the Phoenix is
                timeless
as gold is

She heads for
        the sky

like a grown child
leaving Mother

leaves the warm ash
resplendent
            above
below

AUDRE LORDE

before you died you went to Mt. Pele
for the solar eclipse

you told me
you had an appointment

with the goddess

the light   the splintered
rocks.   storms that rearrange
the coastline—this is my home.

I take refuge here.

FOR SHEPPARD
(Healer & Beloved)

now I cook the "tree-bark gruel" for myself
w/ the same love
w/ which you cooked it for me

letting me know I'm worth it:
the time, the care, the
(sometimes rare) ingredients

and I wonder as I stir
the strange stuff—almost alive—
whether that isn't what you do
for everyone you

"work on"
            Letting them know
as you chant the purifying mantra
touch the crown of their heads
as it hasn't been touched
since they were new-born
(if then)

letting them know
they are worth all care
all tenderness

they are gold of the gold
so precious   carry the Source

it bubbles   a luminous spring
thru every cell   of their
sickly,   tired bodies

wind chime sends ripples
thru the sphere of clear light

in which I have just taken refuge

THE LAMA

the crystal
       he held it
never stops
         reflecting
doesn't
        get tired

he turned it
              caught the
light   replaced it

in a bowl of rice

his hand
        trembled slightly

THREE DHARMA POEMS
for Chogyam Trungpa Rinpoche

1.
his vision or not?
gone is the authority
w/which he opened his fan.

2.
raindrops melt in the pond
& it's hard to say
just what "lineage" is

3.
my faith—
what is it
but the ancient dreams

of wild ones
in the mountains?

A HEALING SPELL FOR MOUSE

one cup of
green light
(healing breath of plants:
live oak in winter rains)

one cup of
blue light
sky in autumn
over the plains

cut into strips & weave
a healing blanket   wrap
the patient in it
wrap Mouse in it and shine

gold light of the sun
thru the blue, thru the green
gold light of summer solstice
at Oraibi

let the four elements
the four directions
DANCE
around him

then mix it up

green Tara, medicine Buddha
arura flower (which cures everything)
kusha grass (for prophetic dreams)
Asklepios, Kokopelli   the Red Stone
of the alchemists, wise heart
of the Grandmothers

wise heart
SUN in his center
SUN shining down

the way it moves
winds dance now
winds
the little winds

he is whole

TAYATA OM

mix it up!

White Tara   Medicine Buddha
arura flower   (which cures everything)
Asklepios   Kokopelli   Red Stone
of the alchemists   Raphael
"Healing of God"   Sapphire *(for*
this stone   giveth sleep)   kind hearts
        of the Grandmothers

warm heart
wise heart

> *SUN in his center*
> *SUN shining down*
> *night SUN shining up*
> *thru center*
> *of the earth*

in the heart of the Void is found the Great Medicine

TAYATA OM!

A FAREWELL RITE
for Peter Hartman

you can put down your drugs now
put down
your fierce lust
only the Light Body travels
east wind
blowing you west toward the dark

put down your fine wines
your cymbals from Sikkim
Light Body rises like mist
from your swollen corpse

[July 1988 AIDS epidemic]

ZORON, YOUR DEATH

you climbed
out of yr hospital bed
when I came for a visit

it was awkward
all those tubes
to arrange,   untangle

you had us place your armchair
so you cd see that tiny patch of sky
walked the four steps by yourself

yr parents
good folks from Nebraska
protested

but you arranged yourself
regal &
looked at the sky
& they decided to walk
to the end of the hall

I sat down beside you
& right away   you asked
what did it mean to Take Refuge?

you were doing it tomorrow
Yeshe, a gay, a tattooed American
                    tulku
was coming to help you become
a Tibetan Buddhist

We had only a minute
I told you what I could:

*Taking refuge in **Buddha** you rest*
        in your own wisdom mind;
*in **Dharma** you trust the suchness*
        of things as they are
*in **Sangha** you join with all beings*
        their essence & yours
        is Way-seeking Mind

I reminded you then   of yr trip
when you came to San Francisco, early '70s
yr friend, a dyke from Omaha, drove you both
to the city of promise

I hoped you'd see yr journey into death
as an even greater Adventure:

                    you beamed at me
yr eyes twinkling & ready   holding mine

yr folks came back then   I said goodbye
went home

next morning I got the call:
                          you had died
before Yeshe got there

                          but I knew
in yr armchair, the day before
when I was with you
looking together into that
                    small patch of sky

you had somehow taken refuge
in all of Space

[September 1992—AIDS Epidemic]

WHERE ARE YOU?

friends know where other friends live
not their emails or cell phone numbers
not something called their "contact information"

if she's a friend
you can show up at her door when you're in trouble
you can mail him your new book when it's finally
"out"

you can drop by when you hear they've got to move
& pack the books while they order pizza and beer
and you rent a van with yr one good credit card

she doesn't say "stay in touch" and mean Facebook
or LinkedIn
stay in touch means you touch each other, lovers or
not
you crash on his floor, or bring her your old sofa
when another friend brings you his because he's
leaving town

it means when you're home from the hospital
he brings a casserole or soup for the freezer
or mops your floor, makes sure you can reach what
you need

stay in touch doesn't mean a touch screen or even an
iPhone
it means she'll drive you to look at the ocean
or say goodbye to your ex
he'll do your shopping or pick up a prescription

it means one of us will stay with your three-year-old
if you have to stay overnight at the hospital
where you just had your second baby

it means you can borrow her car; get it back to her
when everything's finally cool; and she'll even
draw you a map of the back way out of town
if you're new to this part of the world

it means you can lay your hands along a face
that's been beautiful so long you don't see even now
the edema, the death in his eyes

have you ever tried to email chicken soup?
make love for the last time on Skype?
or give that one more hug before the train leaves
by reaching all the way out through cyberspace?

my dream of last night
has been lying in wait all day
in the folds of my pillow

TRAVEL POEM FOR SHEP

leaving on a ten day trip
I get back in bed
for the warmth & to feel
your body against mine

when the time comes
how will I leave this world

at once & without
looking back?

EYE CLINIC WAITING ROOM

I greet old poet friend

he touches
my hand on his shoulder

whispers
Can you still read?

OLD AGE: The Dilemma

most of what I'm writing
       not that interesting
but the act of writing itself

more compelling than ever

SOME WORDS ABOUT THE POEM

Poetry can bring joy, it can ease grief. It bridges different worlds & myriad cultures.

Poetry can bring rain & make the crops grow. It smoothes the path for the traveler and brings sleep to the feverish child.

Poetry is our heart's cry and our heart's ease. It constantly renews our seeing: so we can speak the constantly changing Truth.

Poets speak truth when no one else can or will. That's why the hunger for poetry grows when the world grows dark. When repression grows, when people speak in whispers or not at all, they turn to poetry to find out what's going on.

Poetry holds the tale of the tribe—of each and every tribe, so when we hear it, we can hear each other, begin to know where we came from.

We write poetry to remember, and sometimes we write poetry to forget. But hidden in our forgetting, encoded there, is our remembering—our secrets.

Poetry holds paradox without striving to solve anything.

Sometimes it speaks the unspeakable.

Always the stream of language points backward toward its source. Toward the moment before speech:

headwaters of the river of language that streams through unfolding worlds.

The poem can be ritual or dance, prayer or dirge. It is music, story, riddle, lullaby. Song, spell, enchantment. Hex or blessing. Serenade or reverie. There is nowhere it can't go, nothing the poem can't be.

The poem is dream and dreamer intertwined. It remakes language in the act of being writ. Mind and tongue, breath and mark. Papyrus, clay, paper, cyber-bit and byte.

When spoken, the poem cuts a shape in time, when written it forms itself in space. It often dwells there in paper or parchment before you pick up your pen. At those times all you have to do is trace what is hidden in the page. At other times you may hear the poem broadcast, spoken like a radio in your head & you can write it down like taking dictation.

And yet it is always, inevitably, rooted in our flesh—the very flesh of the poet who writes or types: *Music begins to atrophy when it gets too far from the dance. Poetry begins to atrophy when it gets too far from music,* a great poet observed. The poem is our breath, our heartbeat.

Poetry brings us together, helps us know one another. It bridges time as well as space—we can glimpse the worlds of

Whoso list to hunt I know where is an hind. . .

Darkling I listen, and for many a time
I have been half in love with easeful Death. . .

though those worlds are long gone. Just as we can
read the poetry of a contemporary thousands of miles
away and feel transported to that place, feel that soil,
that sun.

At a reading for the Sandinistas long ago, my son
Rudi said: *All artists are warriors, aren't they, Mom?*
That's because there's so many parts to art.